LET ME LICK YOUR MIND
"Deeper"
SECOND EDITION

Joanne "*BlackPoet*" Stephen

Let Me Lick Your Mind
"Deeper"
Second Edition
Copyright © 2025 Joanne Stephen

All rights reserved. This is a fiction book. Any resemblance to any person, dead or alive, is purely coincidental. No part of this book can be replicated or duplicated without reference to the book. No part of this book may be stored in a retrieval system, database, and or published in any form or by any means, electronic, mechanical, photocopying, recording, or otherwise, without the prior written permission of the author and or publisher.

ISBN: 979-8-218-74378-9

Joanne "BlackPoet" Stephen
https://linktr.ee/AuthorBlackPoet

Email:
Stephenjbp2@gmail.com

Cover Design & Interior Design by:
Carlos V. Kaigler/ C'vaughn'K Graphic Designs/ Author The Poet
B.GKL
www.authorbgkl.com

LET ME LICK YOUR MIND
"Deeper"
SECOND EDITION

Let Me Lick Your Mind "Deeper" Second Edition

Let Me Lick Your Mind

Contents

My Ink Is Not For The Weak 2
You Make Me Sick 4
Carried Away 6
Captive Thoughts 7
Wrongly Accused 8
Skeletons 10
No Apologies 11
Our Kids Need Help 12
Be Ready 14
Your Shoes 15
Profiling 16
She Smoked Them 18
Finish Me 20
Drop Those Tears 22
I'm Pregnant 24
The Instrument 25
Are You His Peace or Problem 26
Heatwave 28
Freedom 30
Missing 32
Rooted 34
That's Not a Butt 35
How Deep Is Her Yoni 37
Colors 38
Just Don't 40
Water Me 42
The Neighborhood 44
Coldest Poem Ever 46
My Truth, Their Lie 48
Game Over 50
Clouded 51
Artwork 53
I Heard Your Silence 54
Fallen Sisters 55
Pieces 58
Fire 60

Feel The Mind Become Licked With The Wit Of Depth!

Let Me Lick Your Mind "Deeper" Second Edition

Poems

Let Me Lick Your Mind "Deeper" Second Edition

My Ink Is Not For The Weak

My ink is not for the weak

I'm telling you it's true

People be in their feelings

So high it's touching the ceiling

I don't just write, it comes from the heart and soul

While some pieces are loving

Others may appear cold

But above all, I know it's the truth

I will be hitting home runs just like Babe Ruth

Far from the candy bar, but I'm just as sweet

Most read my work like a delectable treat

I'm not bragging, just thankful

What can't be said will be written in full

I thank God for this ink, which is my link

That keeps my lifeline going

This is what I'm grateful for, and my work that I will continue showing

My pen is like a smoking gun

I take it seriously, this is not for fun

I will make sure to hit your head space

Then let it trickle down to put a smile on your face

My ink is not for the weak

Let Me Lick Your Mind "Deeper" Second Edition

I may scare the Christians and intrigue the freaks

But it's all good, my ink led me to new friends

And at this time in life, it's the best trend

—Blackpoet

Let Me Lick Your Mind "Deeper" Second Edition

You Make Me Sick

Over the years, everything was good

But now everything is misunderstood

I can't trust anything you say

You're just another pigeon with a message to relay

You are poisoning us slowly

With a mask that appears to be friendly

I don't know who you are

Just another pusher by far

Someone to wear a science coat

To try a new drug, they want to promote

Using us as a guinea pig

With your phony methods in our pockets, you dig

You make me sick

Giving out vaccines like cheap clothes from ***SHEIN***

They are only wishing for population control

Sterilizing our young kids and eliminating the old

There's a warm place for you and your friends to dwell

So, pack your bags lightly as you rot in hell

Having these drug dealers give us garbage to suppress one thing and raise many others

They start from birth and go all the way to our grandmothers

No one is safe, as they make us sick

Purposefully generating new viruses to see which one will stick

How do you live with yourselves and sleep at night

No care in the world because the money is just right

Karma has a friend known to be a bitch

She never discriminates; she gets the old and the rich

Money can't buy eternal life

What you have planned for us can hit your family or your wife

I'm over being healthy with their need to prick

Because after they're done, they just make me sick

-Blackpoet

Carried Away

I love being carried away by my King
His strong arms and legs support my frame
He puts me over his shoulders with ease
I'm like drapery clinging to his skin
That warm, dark chocolate feels so good against my skin
His smell is so divine, I just want to swim in his essence
I'm not only carried away by him physically, but mentally too
I get such a light feeling with thoughts of him
No stress on my cranium
My protector, lover, and provider
My genie makes my dreams come true
My King, who was made perfectly for me
How can I not be carried away?

-Blackpoet

Captive Thoughts

I can't break free out of my mind

The negative thoughts keep me captive

As much as I try, they take me over

I remember all the hurt and pain

Damaged

Not even the craziest of glues can put me back together

I'm broken

Cracks everywhere, including my face

I can't even form a smile

Jailed by my thoughts, no one can save me

I can barely save myself

Happiness is a mask I use in public

I'm surrounded by darkness

Naked to my truth

One day, I hope to be free of my captive thoughts

And live life

-Blackpoet

Let Me Lick Your Mind "Deeper" Second Edition

Wrongly Accused

I'm a tall black man, pretty clean cut
Always smelled good when my wife slapped my butt
A hard-working father 6 days a week
I'd make a little extra money for odd jobs I would seek
Never at a strip club, never at a bar
Always remained local, never ventured too far
Yet one night, my life took a turn
Everything I worked for, I lost, as you will learn
It's walking the streets as a black man
All it took was a pointed finger, and I was in a corrections van
My life was swept off my feet
Being accused by someone I have never met
An uncanny resemblance taken late at night
Because a woman and her man got into a fight
He shined her face pretty well
As I looked at her briefly and saw her eyes swell
I pleaded to say it wasn't me
But she insisted, and the cops would soon agree
So many years of my life, I have had to fight inside
Lord knows how many days I sat and cried
While I missed my wife and family too

How many men are locked up for things they didn't do
Years have passed, and I'm released to a world I don't know
I barely escaped being on death row
Because the man they thought was out on the street
When the truth comes out, it's bittersweet
I lost so much, and I was mentally abused
All because of one night, when I was wrongly accused

-Blackpoet

Skeletons

The skeletons in the shadows, we all carry a few

Some deal with them daily

While some have lost their view

The skeletons in your closet truly never die

Just buried deep enough so you wouldn't have to cry

But if you dwell on them long enough, they will reach the surface

But by the time you've realized it has served no purpose

For the skeletons in our closets were all learning lessons

If you didn't learn from them, that's why you'll stifle your life's progressions

-Blackpoet

Let Me Lick Your Mind "Deeper" Second Edition

No Apologies

Why do I need to apologize?
When it was my life, you tried to jeopardize
You thought I wouldn't realize
The jealousy I saw within your eyes
Apologize or what
Every woman you passed by you watched her butt
You tried to punch me in my gut
This is why it's your ass I had to cut
No apologies from me
You're filled with misery
I'm glowing with glory
You can't see me happy
Apologies from me, you must be crazy
What's your name again?
Oh, it must be memory
I have none for you
That's why my skies remain blue
I'm done with this show, it's a real comedy
You can die waiting because there's no apology

—Blackpoet

Our Kids Need Help

There is no motivation with the students today

They care about nothing anymore; the girls don't even slay

They come to school in pajamas and bonnets and think that it's cool

But they don't realize how they look like a fool

The same clothes they sleep in are the same ones they walk with in the streets

Dust on their pants and dirt in their sheets

I mean, both the boys and girls, that's all they wear

Looking and smelling terrible, and they don't even care

Their underarms can put you in a headlock

Their breath will have you go into shock

No matter how pretty or handsome they may appear

The odor and stench make it all clear

Our kids need help, and they are going through a lot

They barely eat food; they just want to smoke pot

Morning, noon, and night

Their high has no flight

They walk around stoned and clueless with no emotion

Filled with anger and ready for a commotion

No inspiration to be anything at all

Just glued to their phones and making TikTok's against the wall
Our kids need help as they will be the future adults
Their minds have no control, like people who join cults
It's a shame to see so much potential be lost
And at the rate they're going, their lives will be the cost

—Blackpoet

Be Ready

It's time to be ready

Information is thrown at us, and it's shady

Plans are being plotted in the dark

So be ready

Our lives may shift, and it will spark a tidal wave of unfiltered feelings

Emotions and situations hitting the ceiling

Open up your eyes, no time to be asleep

Our allies have put castrations on our nation

As we look like a bunch of clowns

Our voices are silenced, votes stolen from us all

While the cheater sits on the highest seat

Be ready in every shape and form

The war is brewing, and it's right in front of our eyes

-Blackpoet

Your Shoes

You left your shoes for me to follow in your footsteps
I was never that desperate and needy
I'd rather walk barefoot than use your shoes
Your footwear is filled with lies and deception
The very thing to steer me in the wrong direction
You failed to realize how headstrong I am
The path I follow is my own
I'm a born leader, and following is not in my vocabulary
So let your funky shoes stay stationary
While I work in my abundance
A word you'll never understand
Not until you change your ways and live right
I won't have time to find out
I'm leaving you and your shoes right here

-Blackpoet

Profiling

They want my money, but don't want me
I paid for my things, yet they still called security
The embarrassing feeling, and everyone staring
They knew I was innocent, but no one seemed to care
Now I gave you a piece of my mind
I'm rude and uncooperative
I take a glance at others, and they are not even supportive
The disrespect for no reason has me ostracized
Since they believe it's true, and that's what I realized
Take your hands off me, I didn't take anything
But if you look to your left, she just stole two rings
Of course, you didn't see
Because you just had your eyes on me
From the point of me walking in, I felt I had a tail
Each and every corner was your trail
Even though I paid for my things in full
Something in your brain said that was bull
So, you checked your cameras, and you checked my bags
You saw everything I paid for with all its tags
I don't need your apology; the damage is already done
As I call my lawyer, I know this case I have already won
Matter of fact, keep your damn clothes

Let Me Lick Your Mind "Deeper" Second Edition

I want my money back

If I see that girl again, I'd tell her to clean off your rack!

-Blackpoet

She Smoked Them

She smoked those bodies left and right
She didn't care if they were black or white
Short or tall, she smoked them all
He appeared to be a damsel in distress
But she had something lethal underneath her dress
She was walking around with a vengeance
Off of one night with her lover in sight
She recalls a few things that linger as the night fades
As he found out that she has AIDS
He knew he had it and didn't tell her
Now, anyone who's in her path has been made to suffer
But she is a danger to society and everyone
Not making it any easier since she has a son
No care in the world smoking them one after the other
Forgetting that there is help, and she's still a mother
Walking around angry in a selfish state
She was mad at everyone except the person who changed her fate
It's ok to be hurt, but not ok to hurt others
She had no protection while he was dipping in other brothers
Unbeknownst to her, that part was left in the dark

He, too, was violated one day in a park
He was too ashamed to tell her
Everything in her life now became a blur
Each and every day, she smoked one
Smoking'em so hard she thought it was fun
She was running through everyone in the community
Giving everyone a taste of her misery
Until one day, one of those she infected told her to come over
She pulled up looking cute in her Range Rover
It was hard to see his face with the blaring sun
She heard a bang, now her spree is done
As she dropped to the floor right above her hem
There was a tattoo there that read, she smoked them

—Blackpoet

Finish Me

You're not going to just take a few bites out of me

Finish me

Enjoy all the sweetness as a whole

Let me suppress your appetite

Bite into the white

You taste that, don't you?

I knew you'd like it

Now, calm down, you're trying to get to the seed

Take your time before you choke

That's it, savor the juices

You have a lot more to go

You thought this was a quick bite

You were sadly mistaken

You were so used to rushing your food, you never enjoyed it

This time, you picked the perfect fruit

Don't let the appearance fool you

It's packed with a punch

I see you grabbing it more

Trying to eat out the core

Eyes rolled back

Juices sliding down your face

Need a tissue?

Here you go, wipe your face

Finish up, you have a meeting to attend to

Next time you see me, just know I'm on the menu

No left overs, finish me

-Blackpoet

Drop Those Tears

My brothers drop those tears, and don't you hide
Feeling pressured by society and your pride
Why should you have to hold it all in
Keeping in all that negative energy like a sin
They tell us it's ok and have a good cry
But for men, it's a weakness, and I don't know why
As if men are robots without any feelings
When we don't know half of their daily dealings
Being strong for their families, treated poorly at work
Constantly being misunderstood, while some act like a jerk
A target for all, they can't remove the bullseye
You have the nerve to say that a man shouldn't cry
I say drop those tears and let it out
Release yourself and scream and shout
There's nothing wrong with removing excess stress
Stop listening to all that foolishness
In my eyes, you can drop those tears and remain strong
I wish someone would say what you're doing is wrong
As if your heart and pain should be dismissed
Keeping it in would only grow like a cyst
Yet they wonder what's wrong with our men
If the roles were reversed, they'd flip, can I get an Amen?

Fellas, drop those tears when you feel the need
Don't bottle up anything and have your heart bleed
We need you out here being and doing your best
And how others judge you, we need to put that to rest

—Blackpoet

I'm Pregnant

The good news is that I'm pregnant

Yes, I am pregnant, a seed has been planted

I'm not sure of the due date as of yet

In the meantime, I will make sure to nourish it well

Give it all the right information so it turns out rich and healthy

So that when I give birth, I'm giving birth to greatness

A great masterpiece filled with knowledge, love, and the purest of emotions

My spilled ink will spread across the paper and into the hearts of many

Leaving all lines filled with glee, passion, and rawness

I will protect it from green eyes and wandering hands

The birth of this masterpiece will impact the world

I smiled and rubbed my head with anticipation

I can't wait until my poetic child is born

—Blackpoet

Let Me Lick Your Mind "Deeper" Second Edition

The Instrument

When you pick her up, it's hard to put her down

Not only mesmerizing in looks, but the sweet sounds can put you in a trance

The way the instrument stands firm in your hands with every movement

Your grip only gets tighter

As you play sweet melodies with her strings, she echoes the most beautiful sound from her vocal cords

The music transcends into an orchestra of love

Having your body and soul move in sync

The music cascading across your body like the Windy City

As the two of you move in harmony

The instrument deletes your deepest sorrows

Filling you with an enormous euphoria

As you masquerade in her symphony

Your musical prelude leads to an abyss of love

Your bodies feel immortal through the song and dance

The instrument that you play gives you an undying desire to keep playing with her strings

And the musical journey continues

–Blackpoet

Are You His Peace or Problem?

Many women are single, no matter how beautiful they may appear
Hair done, nails done, body done, and complaints are all you can hear
Why am I single? Why doesn't he want me?
Any man would see me and consider himself lucky
But what you fail to realize it's more than looks for these guys
Are you more concerned with what he wears and drives?
Or will you back him when he's at his lowest to thrive
Do you always need to have the last word?
Or keep chirping in his ear like an annoying bird
Are you his peace or are you his problem?
You can see him every day, but that won't solve them
A man is more than a penis and a wallet, a phrase most women ignore
They are too caught up trying to front for their friends wearing Prada, Gucci, and Dior
Can you build his confidence and treat him like a King?
Or do you wait to throw his darkest secrets at him in the ring?
Since that's the only way you feel you can win a fight

But ask yourself this: Do you think it's right?

Men were taught to be strong, but we tend to forget they have feelings too

They have enough on their hands and don't want to come home dealing with you too

Are you his peace or his problem?

Can you listen silently with your full attention?

Or are you leaving him hanging in suspension?

Take your time to know your man, and maybe things will be better

Instead of a couch potato, he'd be a go-getter

When there is peace in his home, he has peace in his dome and will treat you like no other

Because you can be beautiful as hell, but if he sees no peace, he won't bother

So don't be so cocky about your appearance when it comes to a man

The thing he wants most is not your body but peace on demand

You'll look at another woman and wonder why he's with her and not you

Because she knows how to be a woman to him, and you can't fill her shoe – *Blackpoet*

Heatwave

Another summer night with this heatwave
It gives her thoughts of the one thing that gets her hot but cools her right down
A smile comes across her face, and she makes that call
Hey baby, what's up besides this heat?
Are you feeling hungry because I have the right treat?
The pipeline is on the way
Dripping wet are the sheets that await his arrival
The freshly mowed lawn just shows the passageway to the heavenly soul
As the excitement draws near, the juices seem to thicken as she sees the arrival of a familiar face
Jackpot, he's going to work as the warmth of his tongue touches her cavity
He spreads her legs so his face can breathe
No interruptions between the two
Just hot, steamy sex in their view
The music he makes as he cascades all over her body
Kissing the tip of her mountains while trying to bring them together
Her heavy breathing indicates she's ready for the pipeline
As he enters her wet garage for a tight yet slippery slope

He groans in ecstasy, and his eyes roll to the back of his head
She too joins in the music as she moans to the movement of the pipe being laid
More sweat drips between them
Outlining the sheets from one position
Only to move into another pounding, away from the satisfaction of clapping those cheeks
This heat wave is far from over as she rides the pipe, his mouth is open, yet he remains quiet
She rides that cowboy until she goes on her toes
Then he starts to fight the trembling feeling
He pounces on her like a rabbit on speed
The thunderous roar between the two is on high alert
As they clench each other's hands, both yelling I'm about to cum
They reached their climax, and the tornado in the room subsided
Only to rise again in this heatwave until they both fall asleep

—Blackpoet

Let Me Lick Your Mind "Deeper" Second Edition

Freedom

(Fu@k, Racism, End Everyone's Doom Over Money)

It's spelled freedom, but freedom for whom?
Definitely not for me, damn well it's not for you
Still slaves with individual shackles
While they sit in their offices, we hear their cackles
Watching everyone like a puppet on a string
Having us like robots to bells and dings
Each day, we walk and work like clockwork
Anything out of line causes people to act berserk
With the chump change dangling in the form of a check
Keeps most of them in order
Building up walls can't even run for the border
The few who venture out they punished
All we hear out of their mouths is rubbish
Punishing folks with unwavering taxes and fees that most
entrepreneurial businesses go quiet
It's enough to make one want to start a riot
Making it harder for people to make ends meet
Some, due to desperation, turn to drugs on the street
Whether using or selling, they are in the game
Just looking to survive very few for the fame
Feeding ammunition in the hood

Because they feel half of them out here are just no good

Not even those who swore to protect and serve

Asking them for help turns into a curve

Where you have to fend for your own

Afraid of being gunned down in your own home

So, where's the protection

It's only for a selection

We never made the list

Some freedom

Yeah, it's dumb to think we are free

In this society, it's not even for those with the highest pedigree

Freedom for some is yet to come, and the only way some are free

It is when they are looking at their lifeless body

I see the red for the blood, the white, who get over with the blue-collar crimes

Made as stars even in the most perverted rhymes

The land of what seems to be a disgrace

Who laughs at our freedom, right in our face

-Blackpoet

Missing

Where are our kids going?
The number of missing children is growing
No one wants to talk about this subject
Why is it happening? Why do they forget
We protect those, whether they're ours or not
Sharing is caring, and sometimes you only get one shot
Our children are missing... doesn't anyone care
All these cameras are around, but they are vanishing in thin air
Someone knows something we can't accept this
It's been happening for too long, and it shouldn't be dismissed
Different pictures are posted on social media
But they can be overlooked quickly by a celebrity having chlamydia
Where are the celebs who can use their influential status?
They, too, have gone quiet into their hiatus
No one seems to care besides their family and friends
Our children are missing, and it's a continuous "trend"
Some are held captive, used as slaves, or traded as we see today
Then there are those that never get to see the light of day

I can't keep quiet since I'm part of the village
Too bad others don't feel the same, trying to protect their image
Well, we need to help and bring these kids home
Look at everything through a fine-tooth comb
Every child deserves the chance to grow up
So, we as adults need to do our part and take a step up
When a child goes missing, it shakes up a community
We have to find more ways to ensure their safety
A missing child does not hurt the family alone
Please let's come together and try to bring these home

—Blackpoet

Rooted

She is deeply rooted in her reds, yellows, and greens
Running through her veins like the water streams
Thick and strong like nature intended
Built for anything thrown at her, with the many hearts she has mended
She is made like no other, while too many try to imitate
From the soles of her feet to the crown on her head, you cannot duplicate
For she is deeply rooted, only those with shared soil will know
That this particular woman is more than a spectacle or show
This divine empress, whose structure is built to withstand any storm
Can be a chameleon in any area of life, and that is just the norm
She must be respected and cherished, not just online or in papers, but in our community
Because when I look at her, I know **SHE** is me!

-Blackpoet

That's Not A Butt

That's not a butt but a pamper you're looking at, you sick freak
Not even old enough to satisfy your mental streak
You have a perverted and twisted mind
Salivating over a child's behind
Who are you, and what is your purpose?
You shouldn't be allowed on the surface
What can a child do for a grown man?
Who still needs the care and love from their parents' hands!
Are you repeating a cycle? Who hurt you?
Leave her breasts alone, were you deprived?
Is this how your sickness arrived?
Let these children be at peace
Not a piece for your sexual playground
That's why you stick around
In the parks and anywhere kids have fun
Don't even look at mine, Cuz' I'm not the one
I'll have you looking down a barrel, and then you're done
Crop tops, miniskirts, fake nails, and hair
Why would you make those things for little girls to wear?

Wandering eyes are piercing their skin, and they are so unaware
I blame some parents who don't pay attention, and others who just don't care
But that's a separate message
You have to watch your surroundings; they are all over
Following kids on their bikes, feet, and rovers
Calling them over to help find your imaginary puppy
Making them promises and offering candy
What a sick world we are in when our kids are not protected
They are in our schools, on TV, and some are even elected
Let's protect our kids and give them a chance to grow
They can be the next big thing, but we will never know
As they keep coming up missing, this needs to stop
Who do you turn to for help when the creeps are on top?
I don't know, but change starts with one
That's all we need for the case to be won
Then maybe more kids will be able to be around
While those freaks are locked up or buried underground
Let the kids be kids, untouched and innocent

-Blackpoet

Let Me Lick Your Mind "Deeper" Second Edition

How Deep Is Her Yoni?

The depth of her Yoni surpasses the pleasure zone

It brings life to where little ones call home

It's the tunnel of love and life

The only tunnel where men lose their minds

In the brim of satisfaction

Yoni is such a valid piece of her anatomy

It sends signals when something is wrong

It's more powerful than you can ever imagine

The depth of her Yoni can stretch for miles

Yet snaps back to its original form

It cradles the passageway to bring forth the most precious beings

The sweetest of fruit many love to eat

How special it is to know how deep her Yoni really is

-Blackpoet

Colors

The color of my skin stays the same
In the sun, it may get a little darker
In the winter, it may appear lighter
Yet I'm still labeled colored, or shall we say black
Others in the summer turn red
When they are cold, they turn blue
Some have been known to turn purple
If you know you're sick, you're green in the face
Yet I'm the colored one
Still feared among many without knowing me personally
I was made from royalty
As they duplicate many
This melanin is loved behind closed doors
Even when the mics are off, the truth is loud and clear
Why does my skin tone cause so much fear?
You compare me against many others of the same
To label me less than until you know my worth
Your eyes dazzle with the dollar signs as you are aware of my richness
Rich indeed from my head to my feet
Colors are for clothing, crayons, and the rainbow
You were taught to see me as darkness

But I'm so close to the light, you need shades

Well, my black is beautiful

My brown is even better

If I had a choice, I'd choose this all over again

Wake up from the hate, as kids, we are colorblind

The only color we saw was red, and that was from all the love

-Blackpoet

Just Don't

The air is not clean, and you may still need to wear a mask

Don't touch that! It hasn't been sanitized, yet we need the public transportation

Don't drink the water, it has skin-eating parasites

Put that back, the meat is no good, it could be digitally made

Don't drink that milk, it's no good for you, and neither are the others

Stay away from a list of foods, as they contain numerous chemicals

Wait! Those fruits have no seeds, even those labeled organic are known to be fake

What now... the new chicken spot is claiming to have human DNA

Is there nothing safe? Did I forget to say *"Please cancel those flights!"*

Too many planes are crashing into each other

Cruise ships that hold hundreds are not properly cleaned

Food sources are tampered with, and the walls are closing in

That bread you just bought appears to mimic a sponge

Don't relax your hair, it may lead to cancer

Let Me Lick Your Mind "Deeper" Second Edition

IS this the life? How can we move on?
Turn the TV off and just don't
Seems like the new reality

-Blackpoet

Water Me

From his loins, I started as a seed to be cooked and nurtured, in my mother's womb, surrounded by water

As she birthed me, I made myself into the world

As I plant my feet into the ground, I still need to be watered

Water me so I can remain grounded and sprout my leaves for shelter and oxygen

I want to continue to be watered as my branches spread wide and broad, to show my strength and resilience

Water me so I'm around for many years to tell many stories, although I stand still

I remain deeply rooted; my trunk is strong, not easily moved

The richness of my color serves as the perfect conversation piece

Rough to the touch but smooth on the inside, many may look the part, but I'm still an original

Water me as my flowers bloom, giving off the perfect scent

Drawing everyone and everything near me, down to the smallest insect

We all have a duty and a reason to be here

So, as I stand tall, I want to be watered so I can be here to
do the job that was embedded deep within me
To be around through the stormy weather and withstand
the highest of winds
I won't break and remain planted
The whispers of my leaves to the smallest of branches will
be here til the end of time
While they grow strong enough to branch out on their own
and tell their tales

—Blackpoet

The Neighborhood

Between the alcohol, the smoke shops, and the Chinese food
All the popping up in our neighborhood puts me in a bad mood
All the poisons get thrown in our area
Our high chances of good food are as slim as getting malaria
The bodegas and gas stations serving you from a box
Getting tired of being robbed, can't afford enough locks
The neighborhood where kids can't play in the park
Especially when the bullets start flying well before dark
Building these complexes, no one can afford
Resulting in multiple people sleeping on cardboard
The drugs are no longer hiding in plain sight
The dealers are just watching everyone high as a kite
Not just those on the corner of the street
You know the big boys are distributing them and the heat
By far, I wish I were talking about the sun
But you know how they're getting those guns
Where can you go without being afraid?
Two blocks from your house, you hear there was a raid
Our kids are not safe, and our elders need help

The supermarkets are trash, can't even get a bunch of kelp
Spoiled meats are stamped with the manager's price
Prices so escalated can't even afford a bag of rice
Outside of the neighborhood, things seem brand new
But the message is clear, it's not for me or you
Everyone is catering to their kind
Living peacefully just blows my mind
Why can't we be the same in our neighborhood?
We should all live in peace from Flatbush to Ridgewood

-Blackpoet

Coldest Poem Ever

The coldest poem ever

When I speak the truth, I'm so clever

When the real history rolls off my tongue

They can't breathe as it pierces their lung

The truth hurts when you swallow it dry

My spilled ink would make their mothers cry

Dropping the coldest poem, and it turns to ice

I'm spitting everything, and I'm not trying to be nice

I'm not acting like a bookworm

But I know my messages make them squirm

Faceless, tactless suckers you never meet

How they hate you silently because you're bringing the heat

I don't have to curse and carry on to bring the message home

Straight fire to the head, having them still like a garden gnome

I could be a lady and keep it discreet

Or let you grab your pillow and hide under your sheet

Because there are times, I need a warning label

When my lyrics get going, my eyes are not able

To keep up with everything I'm saying

Some are funny, but most times I'm not playing

The coldest poem ever written is every day

Once my pen is locked and loaded, you better duck as I spray

—Blackpoet

My Truth, Their Lie

When I speak my truth, knowing it's their lies, you get blocked

Silenced

You spread this lie to infect so many others

Weakened souls

Yet when the truth surfaces from one person, it creates discomfort

Why?

Does it irritate your soul that not all of us are asleep?

Do you have a burning sensation?

That truth pill is hard to swallow

As it passes your esophagus, you feel the need to choke

No water for you, feel the discomfort

My truth keeps me light as if a weight has been freed

So many others were enlightened by the knowledge

Hitting the cerebellum just right, in order to straighten your posture

You can't believe how far the lies go

As you realized how you accepted them for so long

Well, the truth has no expiration date

When the awakening arises, you can't stop the flow

You can only end the lies entering your system

Wearing your armor
No longer having the poison marinating your soul or your next move
Step outside the box, the truth has been told
You'll see it for yourself
You are no longer blinded
As the truth pursues to present itself
The wave will continue nonstop

-Blackpoet

Game Over

It's game over, yall kids play too much
You act like you're so bad that no one can touch
A social media gangster, showing off your guns and knife
Until you met the wrong one who took your life
Was it even worth it? No, it was not
Arguing over nonsense now, there are candles in your spot
Stop playing these deadly games, it's real out here in these streets
Tired of parents burying their kids and having to identify them through bloodstained sheets
When are you going to act your age?
Too many of you are walking around with so much rage
You need to find the root of your problem
Before it's too late and no one can solve them
Having a bad attitude is not good to show
It either results in a heinous beating or a tag on your toe
You weren't born with a four-leaf clover
So, stop this foolishness now before it's game over!

—Blackpoet

Clouded

Clouded with everything, including the lies

Can't even fly over the friendly skies

No privacy anywhere you go

Say cheese to the cameras on a constant flow

You're not even safe in your own house

Everything can be heard, including a mouse

Those smart devices are listening and watching everything we do

Including those intimate moments meant only for two

Cloudy with this AI reality

We are clouded, so we don't see the real reality

Clouded on the board game, just like Monopoly

Yes, Monopoly, so close to the word manipulate

If you see this with me, we called checkmate

We are not dancing anymore, to their buzzers and the rings

They want to keep us clouded like puppets on a string

Wandering aimlessly in their direction

We have to stop them right here and be free from their infection

The infections of towing their lines

Clouding our vision and tampering with our minds

Only some see clearly, but the room is not crowded

Because the masses out here are still walking around, clouded

—Blackpoet

Let Me Lick Your Mind "Deeper" Second Edition

Artwork

I am the artwork; I am the truth and the lyrics

I am built to create and withstand many storms

Tall and statuesque and deeply rooted

The artwork was made with love

A piece to leave you breathless

A chameleon in any room, while outstanding in any crowd

Not easily forgotten, an embedded piece in your cranium,

and quite pleasing to the eyes

Richness in my skin, I am the artwork

My full lips have told the sweetest stories, while my big,

bright eyes have seen great portions of the world

I am the artwork when my hair changes with my mood

The styles embody the nature in which I was created

While emulating my roots and culture, I am the artwork

Many may see me, but can't touch me, a work of art God

has created

A work that will continue to spread love, either by voice or

my written craft

I am the artwork and I am priceless!

—Blackpoet

I Heard Your Silence

I disappeared for a moment; you never looked for me
But if I posted a picture, you'd say I look so pretty
You claim to be a friend, but you never bothered to see
what happened
My page stayed silent for weeks at a time
Not a text or message in my timeline
I hear your silence loud and clear
Who stays on my page watching my every move
The first to comment before the message is done
The one who likes my pictures, almost every last one
But once I got silent, you didn't show a care
Yes, you, that FB friend who is always there
The one peeping with nothing to share
I'm ok, though I needed a moment to see
That **YOU** are not a friend to me
You climb into my inbox for frivolous talk
Now my fingers would tell you to walk
My real friends have already reached out
Your silence just told me what you're really about
So, the next time I hear your silence
It's because you're blocked and deleted!

Fallen Sisters

What happened to our fallen sisters?

Whose crowns seem to be lost!

They crave attention and complain when their needs are not met

What happened to the women who had a mystery?

Now they walk the streets half-naked, leaving everything out to see

I can't find a good man, it seems you never figured out why

That good man probably saw you and passed you right on by

Too turned off by your looks, no matter how pretty you may be

He mentally separated himself from you as your choice of clothing made you ugly

He may have looked in your direction, but not for the reasons you think

His thoughts labeled you deplorable, and to look the other way

A true Queen wouldn't dress that way

You will only be for a good time, but never a long time

You'd be one for the streets, but never bring home

My fallen sister, you *CAN* rise again!
Grown women dressing as children, and children dressing like grown women
The message is contaminated
The fall has spread, leading to a lack of leaders
While leaving the door open for more disrespect
Is this what you call being liberated?
Remember, no one wants the fruit that every hand has touched
As people look at you with laughter and shame
Giving you a name not fit for the Queen, so that you can be
But because you choose to be a sewer rat, it stays with you in the alleys
Calling men thirsty as you showcase your Assets
The so-called fashion is designed to humiliate and degrade you
The plan is in place, and you feel deep in it
While the clowns that surround you can't help you while you call them friends
Crabs in a barrel mentality, where misery meets company, they don't want you to rise above them
My fallen sister change is here with your name on it
The reflection is positive if you give it a chance

Your crown can be straightened, and you can find that romance

Dust yourself off and start over

Your DNA is not meant to be stuck, but to rise forward with Pride, wisdom, dignity, and success

Let anything formed to keep you down never prosper

Turn your circle into a box so those who don't belong can hit those corners

You are worthy if you give yourself the respect, and when you do, others will follow

You are not everyone's pleasure dome, so stop painting that on your canvas

—Blackpoet

Pieces

We live in a world where people want pieces

It can be a side piece, show piece, timepiece, or even a piece of that KitKat bar

But the one we all have experienced is a piece of our hearts

You see many people come as pieces to your puzzle, but they don't fit in

Some pieces are close to what you may need, but it's still not a match

Yet you wondered why it didn't work after you forced it in a place it wasn't meant to be

That piece was not for you, but you tried to make due, and the only piece they caught was the piece from you

Your inner peace is now in pieces

A piece of you that's not easily replaced, so you're on to the next

Some people don't care what kind of piece they get, that's why they stay on the side

You guessed it… the side piece, also known as the showpiece, but not a valuable timepiece

As this specific one tends to be a taker and not a giver

It can be male or female, no one in specific

For most men, it can be terrific as they lay down the pipe,

no need to wipe, another one is just in his sight

As for the female, she'll stay cute for another brute

If you pay for her hair and nails, no great relationship will

prevail, and it's another useless piece that will cost you and

fail

For me, the only piece I need is inner peace

Nothing in this world is better than that

I'm in a calm state of mind; no problems are extra pieces

lagging behind

My peace is the richest thing... Oh My!

But don't be fooled, I still want a piece of that pie from the

big bag, and that's no lie!

—Blackpoet

Fire

OMG, here we go, where do I begin?
No matter can put out my fire from within
The lyrics I speak have heat like a dragon
Shots fired so hard it sounds like my magnum
My poetry is hot and deep, even for my books
The pages are blazing; I see it all in their looks
My words are hot, whether you hear them or read them in your head
I see the smoke coming out as you rise out of bed
My gift within me is the best of me
I don't need anything, not even therapy
I can take you to the streets or straight to ecstasy
I'm telling you the truth, I'm no liar
Spikes are flying like a live wire
Putting some to shame while others retire
Giving it to you as it comes from the top
I can go some more, but for now I'll stop
I just wanted to let some air out of my tire
To warm you up with some of my fire

—Blackpoet

Let Me Lick Your Mind "Deeper" Second Edition

Let Me Lick Your Mind "Deeper" Second Edition

I hope that this secondary edition of pages has **"licked"** your mind much ***DEEPER***, in ways you've never dreamt. Many thanks to my friends and family who have continued to encourage and support me through another grand poetic journey. I truly value your love, support, and time, I want you to know I appreciate you for being the wonderful person that you are. Thank you.

Sincerely,

ABOUT THE AUTHOR

Joanne "BlackPoet" Stephen is a dynamic poetic genius from Brooklyn, N.Y. The diverse creative approach invested in her writings carries fluid themes. Joanne's execution of life and expression in print uniquely connects as well as compels in meaningful ways. She's also the author of ***Through My Eyes*** and ***The Insights of BlackPoet. Let Me Lick Your Mind*** is a masterful, engaging, timely, and informative piece that is sure to stimulate conversations for generations to come.

Let Me Lick Your Mind *"Deeper"* is an indulgent, inviting conversational list of poems. My goal is to allow words to feed the mind with a mature essence; it will be an intriguing read that will always leave you bewitched, satisfied, and placed into a profound stillness with a reflection of deep thought licked slowly by the life of my pages.

Joanne "Black Poet" Stephen

Let Me Lick Your Mind "Deeper" Second Edition

www.ingramcontent.com/pod-product-compliance
Lightning Source LLC
Chambersburg PA
CBHW050705160426
43194CB00010B/2012